THE TEMPLES OF JAVA

Y0-CBU-024

THE TEMPLES
OF JAVA

Jacques Dumarçay

Translated and edited by
MICHAEL SMITHIES

SINGAPORE
OXFORD UNIVERSITY PRESS
OXFORD NEW YORK

Oxford University Press

Oxford New York Toronto
Petaling Jaya Singapore Hong Kong Tokyo
Delhi Bombay Calcutta Madras Karachi
Nairobi Dar es Salaam Cape Town
Melbourne Auckland

and associates in
Beirut Berlin Ibadan Nicosia

OXFORD *is a trademark of Oxford University Press*

© *Oxford University Press Pte. Ltd. 1986*
First published 1986
Second impression 1987

All rights reserved. No part of this publication may be reproduced,
stored in a retrieval system, or transmitted, in any form or by any means,
electronic, mechanical, photocopying, recording or otherwise,
without the prior permission of Oxford University Press

ISBN 0 19 582595 0

Printed in Malaysia by Peter Chong Printers Sdn. Bhd.
Published by Oxford University Press Pte. Ltd.,
Unit 221, Ubi Avenue 4, Singapore 1440

Contents

Figures

Colour Plates

Black and White Plates

Introduction

ARCHITECTURE is a way of expressing people's desires, giving the form that is desired to space. While this ambition can be found in the most modest dwelling, the temple is its most perfect expression. For all religions, space is the essential manifestation of divine creative powers. The temple raises a minute portion of the earth to superior importance, and is, by this fact alone, apart from any other symbolism, a proof of divine presence.

The spread of the major Indian religions to Java during the first centuries of the Christian era caused buildings to be constructed where religious rites could be performed. We know nothing of the early temples; they must have been built according to architectural canons deriving from southern India, as subsequent constructions show. These later temples, whether built for Hindu or Buddhist rites, corresponded to an architectural scheme which had to reconcile three requirements: firstly, religious ceremonial demands had to be fulfilled; secondly, religious statuary had to be protected; and lastly, a particular symbolism had to be demonstrated. The rites were of two kinds: the form of respect which had to be shown to the principal statue, and the requirement to move around the temple in the traditional manner. The iconographic needs in a Sivaite temple required cruciform plans, allowing the four main statues to be correctly located: Siva in the centre, Agastya (probably another form of Siva) on his right, Ganesha his son behind him and on his left his wife Durga. These requirements were already well established from the time of the building of the Gedong Songo temples at the beginning of the eighth century and hardly changed before the thirteenth century. This was not the same with Buddhist iconography, which changed considerably with time, being most likely affected by complex mandalas which led to very diverse plans.

The symbolism of the temple is not clearly expressed by architecture, which remains completely abstract. The building is above all the dwelling of the god, and is described as such in epigraphic inscriptions. For example, in the important inscription of AD 856, commemorating the consecration of Prambanan temple, the building is described as 'a beautiful dwelling for the god' (J. G. de Casparis, *Prasasti Indonesia II*, Bandung, 1956, p. 323). The gods live on Mount Meru, the central mountain of the universe, around which the stars move. The temple could therefore be assimilated to this mountain (this is made explicit in Khmer epigraphy where buildings are sometimes referred to as 'golden mountains' or 'king of the mountains').

The temples of Java were built within narrow technical, economic and aesthetic constraints which in combination restricted architectural expression.

The buildings to be found in the temple reliefs of Borobudur, Prambanan and East Java show that a great number of religious buildings were made of wood. Given the fragile nature of this material, none of these structures have survived, but the influence of beamwork on architectural form was profound. It gave rise to stone or brick structures poorly adapted to such materials. Nevertheless, in the course of time, techniques appropriate to stone and brick were developed, but until the fourteenth century elements of beamwork employed in stone or brick structures can be seen incorporated in the architectural design.

Stone, most often andesite, was at first used without a binder, with special cuttings giving very good cohesion to the whole, but from the beginning of the ninth century a mortar made of lime, sand and water was used, with rather poor assembly methods. Bricks, in varied forms, were generally well fired and of good quality, but the conditions in which they were dried did not produce very smooth surfaces. As a consequence of this, the bricks were rubbed against each other before being laid. This method gave very good adherence to the layer as a whole and was improved by a binder made from the sap of plants. Although these techniques were sometimes used with ingenuity, they did not allow for bridging broad entrances between two walls, and above all, after the ninth century, the absence of liaison in the internal mass, which was often of considerable size, caused strong pressure on the facings of the base and led to a number of structural failures.

Economic constraints certainly played a large role in temple design. Fiscal exemptions are sometimes mentioned in inscriptions and allow for the maintenance of the building and the performance of religious ceremonies. Land and rice fields incorporated in the temple's domain were completely exempt from tax, not only for the present but for all time in the future. Indo-Javanese epigraphy is not absolutely specific about the financing of buildings; however, it is certain that the wealth and size of the buildings varied according to the importance of the people who ordered their construction. For example, the thirteenth stanza of the inscription of 856, already mentioned, indicated that only the main temple at Prambanan was built by the king. The sanctuaries of the second precinct, which were required to be of equal height and uniform in conception, but which could be different in detail, were most likely built to order by important persons in the kingdom. The numerous small temples scattered throughout the Javanese countryside, of which only the foundations remain, were very modest buildings, put up by village authorities with limited means, even though the inscriptions associated with these temples refer to the king who participated in a remote way with the inauguration of the shrine. The persons commissioning these temples probably did not call in a renowned master builder, who was capable of invention, but rather had recourse to a practical mason who could build according to established canons and who could be sure of making the temple worthy of the god it was built to receive.

In this way the first architectural treatises appeared, normalizing buildings known to have pleased the gods. None of these written works have come down to us in Java, but many exist in India, unfortunately of relatively recent compilation (the earliest dates from the fifteenth century). These texts give almost no technical details, but specify the forms of the outlines of buildings, suggesting a series of carved outlines with specific proportions between each, and described according to a module which had to be fixed in value before beginning the construction. This allowed the formulae to be used whatever the volume of the projected temple. So on temples of very different height the same succession of carved outlines in different scales can be found. These treatises also gave rise to architectural perspective effects, by fixing the proportions of different elements in relation to each other. In reality, neither the techniques nor the economic means existed to allow the fabulous dimensions of Mount Meru to be approached, so the master builders resorted to artifice so that a building would appear bigger than one which they could in fact build. These visual tricks are based on the use of diminishing perspective. If similar elements are diminished proportionally, they appear further away from the foreground than in fact they are. The devotee, on going into the shrine, appeared before an abstract image, formed of different known architectural elements, sometimes recalling wooden buildings. The enlarged representation of these buildings supported the symbolism, indicated by the texts and rites, without it being clearly expressed in architecture.

In spite of epigraphic texts, it is difficult to reestablish the historical context in which Javanese temples were constructed.

They were, nevertheless, not only the dwelling of the god but also a political manifestation. The success of Indian religions was due to their ability to provide existing minor principalities (which came into existence in all likelihood because of the need to organize irrigation) with a framework in which the prince found a further justification for his power. The exaltation of the creative force of Siva, which in a way was a continuation of megalithic religions, was also that of the king, a reflection of the divinity with which he will be merged after his death. In the Buddhist context, the king is a Bodhisattva, a future Buddha, who watches over the well-being of his subjects.

The construction of a temple, Buddhist or Hindu, was an important political act, because it was also an ideal arrangement of the kingdom. This transpires in two similar ways in epigraphic inscriptions and architectural construction. For example, two identical inscriptions were put up in 850 at the time of the inauguration of Candi Perot, a small temple in the region of Temangung. After the name of the king and a list of dignitaries who took part in the ceremony, there is another text connected with the village authorities—the elders, the supervisors of the markets, of irrigation works, everyone who contributed to daily life in the villages. Each is named according to a particular hierarchy, probably somewhat idealized, of the village reality. On a completely different scale, the temple at Prambanan represents a similar ideal, but at the level of the whole kingdom. The adjacent temples were built by persons of rank who left their titles painted on the buildings (or engraved, in the case of Plaosan, which is a temple of the same kind). The positioning of these titles on each level, one higher than the other, should also show their ideal hierarchy around the dead king reincarnated in the statue of the god, and indicating a world he would have liked to have been in during his life.

Javanese temples are also documents describing in their own way the historical evolution of the country. The central part of

Java, in the middle of the eighth century, was divided into two cultural spheres: the south was Buddhist and governed by the Sailendra dynasty, and the north was Hindu under the Sanjaya (this was very tentatively proposed by J. G. de Casparis in *Prasasti Indonesia I*, Bandung, 1950). From 778, the date of the construction of the first Buddhist temple at Kalasan, a constant increase in Buddhism can be observed, culminating in the first years of the ninth century with the completion of the third state of Borobudur. The reaction of the Hindu dynasty to this can be seen around 830, when Buddhist expansion stopped and the construction of the complex of Hindu temples of Prambanan (finished in 856) was undertaken near the biggest Buddhist temple in the region, Candi Sewu. A whole series of small Sivaite temples were also built on the frontier area which had previously separated the two cultural spheres: these include Candi Perot, which has already been mentioned, and also Candi Pringapus and Candi Kuning.

The architecture also demonstrates the great tolerance of the Sanjaya with regard to Buddhism. At the time when the Sanjaya were striving to reunite Central Java, they received from India a new cultural and technical impetus and on a number of Buddhist monuments; contemporary additions, resulting from the reunification and this fresh impetus, can be seen. The Sanjaya, when enlarging Borobudur or reconstructing the entrance to Candi Mendut, wanted, it would seem, to reconcile the conquered Buddhist elements. The Sanjaya ruler Rakai Pikatan did more. On the ruins of an old temple, he constructed the Buddhist complex of Candi Plaosan, but he followed a special concept very close to that of Prambanan. This was the first step towards syncretism which had such success in the thirteenth and fourteenth centuries, but it was also the last large Buddhist temple to be constructed.

For reasons which remain obscure, in the beginning of the tenth century King Sindok moved the capital to the east, to a site which has not been located. This period is very poor in architectural remains, probably reflecting the weakness of the central authority. Nevertheless, there are places where fragments of tenth century Chinese ceramics have been found; this shows that there were plenty of sites in this period, but they were of modest scale. There existed in Java a kind of equilibrium between the central authority and the power of village authorities, and there was movement from one to the other. When the central power was predominant, large enterprises multiplied, but they disappeared when the almost autonomous villages gained the upper hand.

At the beginning of the thirteenth century, when the Singosari kingdom (1222-1292) was established, power had been sufficiently consolidated and architectural constructions were started, though they were never to reach the scale of those of the eighth and ninth centuries. These were the temples directly linked to the dynasty, like Candi Kidal or Candi Jago, which contained the funerary statues of the kings or deceased dignitaries.

In the fourteenth century, after the foundation of the Majapahit dynasty, two changes are to be found in the works of master builders. A certain number of architectural elements lost their abstract character embodying many interpretations, and took on a precise aspect in a more explicit spacial organization. This was underlined by contemporary accounts. For example, the *Negarakertagama*, the chronicle of the court of King Rajasanagara, written in the form of an extended poem by a court official, includes a description of the palace and the capital of King Hayam Wuruk (1350-1389). But, above all, it seems that the master builders had acquired very summary notions of perspective, not only in order to enlarge their buildings as previously, but also to anticipate the way in which the completed work would be viewed. This is clear from the way the upper parts of Candi Pari and Candi Gunung Gansir were constructed as will be explained. The change of attitude in relation to architecture, which could have led to so many developments and allowed the builders to move beyond the architectural canons, was stopped on the one hand by an ever more demanding symbolism which led to Candi Sukuh and Candi Ceto, in the fifteenth century, and on the other by the progress of Islam, the triumph of which obviously brought to an end all Hindu and Buddhist construction in Java.

Hindu Temples to the Beginning of the Ninth Century

THERE are no archaeological remains of temples in the Indianized states in Java before the fifth century. The earliest signs of temple building are in the form of four inscriptions of King Purnavarman, ruler of Taruma in the Jakarta region. They are written in Sanskrit and carved in an alphabet very similar to that used by the Pallava dynasty which reigned at the time in southern India. Although no construction from Purnavarman's time, or that of his immediate successors, has survived, it is reasonable to suppose that temples built in this period owed a lot to the architecture of southern India and that most of them were built of wood. Many representations of those buildings have come down to us on the reliefs at Borobudur. An example is given in Figure 2 (Colour Plate 4): it is found on the third gallery on the north side, and shows a wooden Buddhist temple built on a stone base. It consists of a cella in which four pillars uphold the central part. But the special interest of this relief lies in the fact that it was altered, at a date impossible to determine. The part showing the panels placed between the pillars was removed and replaced by a representation of two high reliefs showing females bearing fly-whisks. This detail was enough to give the appearance of a stone temple to the whole relief. It shows the link between wooden and stone architecture, which can also be seen in the buildings on the Dieng plateau.

'Dieng' means 'the place of the gods' and the temples there can be divided into two groups. The first comprises those buildings from the very last years of the seventh century to about 730, namely Candi Arjuna (Plate 1), Semar (Plate 2),

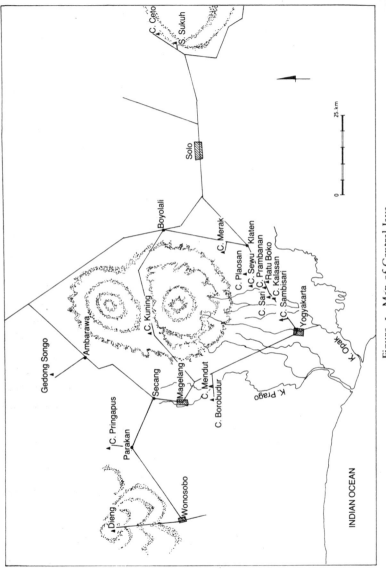

Figure 1. Map of Central Java

0   20 cm

Figure 2. Borobudur, building shown on a relief, third gallery, north side

Srikandi and Gatokaca. 'Candi', incidentally, means 'ancient shrine'; both temples proper and ancient bathing places are grouped together under the blanket term. The actual names of the temples in Java were all, with a few exceptions (Borobudur

12

1. Candi Arjuna (Dieng), south side

2   Candi Semar (Dieng), east side

being one), given to the monuments at the end of the last century or the beginning of this and have no connection with the original name of the buildings.

The second group at Dieng comprises the temples built between 730 and 780, namely Candi Puntadeva, Sembrodo and Bima. This division is a purely formal one, since the site was occupied for a long time; a carved inscription was found at Dieng dating from 1210 and it would appear that for five centuries the temples were changed as evolution in ritual required. This is clearly seen at Gatokaca, where, probably in the middle of the ninth century, the base was enlarged to accommodate a second shrine to the south of the original building. This building was constructed from the level of the infill of the base and, as a consequence of its weak foundation, is now a total ruin.

The temples of Candi Arjuna and Semar form a whole, given over to the cult of Siva, and were probably the first to be built at Dieng. Candi Arjuna had a linga which was ritually bathed on several occasions each day. Water used in the ceremony was carried outside by a gutter going through the north wall and ending in a gargoyle in the form of a makara head, a sea monster with an elephant's trunk (Figure 3). Candi Semar, which is turned towards the west front of Candi Arjuna, probably contained a statue of the bull Nandin, the mount of Siva. This type of temple, unique among those surviving at Dieng and very rare in Java, is similar to the Pallava temples of the seventh century. In spite of the distance in time between Purnavarman's reign and the construction of Candi Arjuna, Javanese master builders were still influenced by the evolution of the Indian model. However, it was also about this period that contact began to be reduced, and the temples built after Candi Arjuna no longer had the gutter carrying away the waste water from the temple ceremonials, which implied a change in ritual.

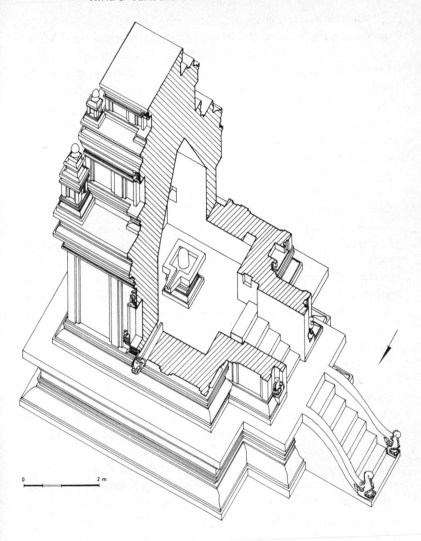

Figure 3. Dieng, Candi Arjuna

Candi Srikandi is decorated with external reliefs, with Visnu on the north, Siva on the east and Brahma to the south. The iconographic arrangement in this way is unusual, but, at Dieng, the rules which eventually governed the construction of temples were not yet well established. This is also obvious at Candi Bima, built on a very different model, probably coming from Orissa, a province in east central India. The master builders designed the temple following a text, possibly illustrated by a drawing, but without direct contact with the original architecture. Each architectural element is represented but on a different scale from those in the temples in Orissa. This attempt, not without its own worth, had no successor.

The temples of Gedong Songo (meaning 'nine buildings': Colour Plates 1 and 2) are scattered over the slopes of a small valley which is formed on the southern side of Mount Ungaran, twelve kilometres from Ambarawa. The different groups of temples are numbered from bottom to top, from one to nine (the ninth has been entirely eroded). The whole complex was built between 730 and 780, except for the first group (Plate 3) which appears to be later, possibly from the beginning of the ninth century. The main shrine in each group was set aside for the worship of Siva, and the other gods in the adjacent shrines are difficult to identify. The northern shrine of the third group contained a Visnu statue and the small shrines to the west of the main temples in groups two, three and six had a statue to Nandin.

It is at Gedong Songo rather than at Dieng that the model of the Javanese Hindu temple was established, with its particular iconography (complete in the main building of the third group), as well as its architecture. By and large these elements were to continue to the thirteenth century. For example, the main temple of the sixth group (Figure 4) has inside a very simple cella opening to the west by means of a narrow corridor ending in a portico. Externally the temple is

3   Gedong Songo, Temple I, east side

1   Foundation
2   Body of building
3   First false storey
4   Second false storey
5   Third false storey
6   Finial or capping
7   Base of main body of building
8   Cornice of the body
9   Portico or porch
10 String walls for approach
    stairway
11 Stepped reduction
    of roofline
12 Pediment

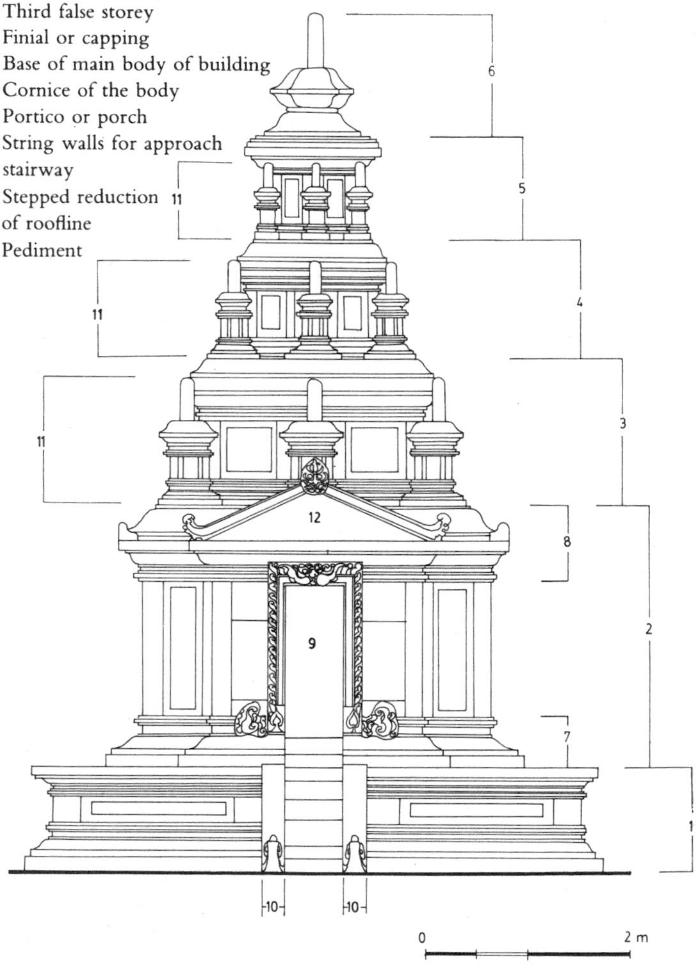

Figure 4. Gedong Songo, group VI, main temple, west side

built on a base which is cut through by a stairway enclosed by low ramps. The portico comprises, on either side of the entrance, a niche which was built for a guardian statue. The other three facades of the body of the building are decorated with pilasters and in the middle is a niche for a statue corresponding to the iconographic representation. Above the body of the building are three false storeys with reductions of the building in decreasing height which, given the effect of perspective, increase the apparent verticality of the building. At this period, a large number of buildings were undoubtedly constructed on this model, not only in stone but also in brick. Unfortunately, most of them have been reduced to a few ruined wall courses.

If East Java is very poor in buildings from this period, it is not entirely without the remains of surviving temples. Near Dau, in the Malang area, a Sivaite temple, Candi Badut, was built around 760. It is very similar to the buildings at Gedong Songo, but the dimensions are notably larger. This shrine must have been considerably altered much later, in the thirteenth century, and this no doubt caused it to collapse.

All these buildings constructed for the cult of Siva in the eighth century are small. However, it is probable that a large temple was projected, but the increasing importance of Buddhism stopped its construction. The first stage of Borobudur, started about 775, uses perspective effects to enlarge the building. This is found nowhere else in Java among Buddhist monuments. The cornice of the first gallery is out of proportion with the height of the wall below it; before the later balustrade was constructed, this would have suggested a larger volume.

For some time, under the influence of Buddhism, Hinduism lost some of its dynamism, which it was not to regain before approximately 835.

2

Buddhist Temples to the Beginning
of the Ninth Century

THE rise of Buddhism in Central Java in the last quarter of the
eighth century led immediately to the construction of a large
number of monuments. This brief period of importance, last-
ing barely fifty years, can be divided into two parts. The first,
from 775 to 790, produced temples with a simple square cella,
with an iconography which is impossible to establish, because
it was entirely replaced in the second stage from 790 to 830. In
this, the temple had a cruciform plan and the iconography
included above all the five Jinas (Vairocana, Aksobhya,
Rathnasambhava, Amithaba and Amaghasiddhi), as well as
other images.

The architectural history of the early Hindu temples in Java
is invariably quite simple, as additions and transformations
were limited to the surrounding complex, the secondary
temples or the entrance pavilions, and the main structure was
not touched. This was not the case with Buddhist architecture,
for every temple was profoundly altered to adapt to religious
evolution and changes in ritual.

The oldest building, remains of which can still be seen,
is Candi Kalasan (Colour Plate 3), in the village of the same
name, ten kilometres from Yogyakarta on the road to Solo.
The first temple on the site was entirely absorbed into subsequent transformations, but the north-west corner has been
excavated and shows a square plan. The temple was devoted
to the cult of Tara and was inaugurated in 778. About twelve
years later, the temple was altered to a cruciform plan, and this
is by and large the monument which can be seen today. The
central cella contains an altar against the west wall; this would

have had a Buddha statue on it, with the legs crossed and seated on a cushion. In the side shrines, on a plinth occupying the whole of the wall opposite the doorway, was a seated statue surrounded by two others of lesser importance, standing or kneeling. The walls of the corridor giving access to the central cella have hollowed in them three niches for standing statues. Externally the monument was also decorated with niches surrounded by foliated scrolls and topped with the head of a monster inserted into the architectural motif. The decoration was first of all carved in stone and then covered with a coating consisting of two parts of lime and three parts of sand, applied in two successive layers. The first was to block the pores in the stone and the second, which at some points is very thick, remained plastic for longer and was suitable for modelling. In this way, the stone sculpture was no more than a kind of guide, more or less complete, for the stucco workers. This was particularly important in allowing the composition of the whole to be kept without any risk of mistakes when alterations were made. Although at Candi Kalasan there are no remains of the covering layers on the scale of those at other temples, it is certain that the carving was covered with stucco.

The roofline comprises, at the first level, a cruciform plan and then on the second and third levels only covers the surface of the cella in the form of two octagonal plans, one smaller than the other. The two octagonal plans were decorated with seated statues representing the Jinas.

The first state of Candi Sewu (meaning 'thousand temples': Colour Plate 6), two kilometres to the north of Prambanan, was laid out at an unknown date, very probably shortly after Candi Kalasan. The temple underwent major changes described in an inscription dating from 792, but this enlargement was carried out in such a way that the original building can for the most part be reconstituted. It comprised in the centre a square building and on the same foundation level four similar

constructions, separate and smaller. Around the main temple was a passageway partially open to the sky to allow for circumambulation. The whole was surrounded by 240 small shrines and the god was everywhere visible (Plate 4).

The first state was not complete before the second started, on a markedly different plan, which probably derived from a drawing of a mandala. Expressed very simply, a mandala is a geometric figure used to enhance the devotee's meditation. When the construction of these geometric figures is sufficiently complicated, small areas are marked out where the names of the gods are inserted and the relationship that exists between them is expressed in this way. Bosch has shown (F. D. K. Bosch, *Selected studies in Indonesian archaeology*, The Hague, 1961, p. 124) that the mandala which was used to establish the plan of the central sanctuary at Candi Sewu was cruciform, and the numerous changes which can be seen in the monument (Figure 5) had no other purpose than to adapt the old structure to new needs. For this, the external niches of the central shrine were incorporated into the side shrines by cutting the circumambulation gallery, but so that this rite could still be carried out, double panelled doorways were inserted. These architectural changes were accompanied by a complete renewal of the statuary. In the central cella, the seated statue was replaced by another, of the same shape but bigger, which involved changes to the altar. This had to be bigger to accommodate the statue. In the side shrines, the groups of three niches had to contain standing statues and the axial niche was changed to contain a seated statue.

Another works programme modified the 240 small shrines. Door casings were inserted and also a porch which partially covered the original decoration. The iconography was no longer constantly visible from the outside and was completely renewed to enhance the classical representation of the five Jinas. Although the number of statues still in place is very

Figure 5. Candi Sewu, schematic restoration of the central shrine

small, it can be seen that their distribution follows a regular orientation. Aksobhya faces east, Rathnasambhava the south, Amithaba the west and Amaghasidhi the north. Vairocana is only shown once, in one of the secondary shrines between the third and fourth row of small shrines.

Candi Sewu is associated with four other temples located approximately on its east-west and north-south axes. To the east the remains of Candi Asu are to be found in the village in front of Candi Sewu. To the north was Candi Lor and the west Candi Kulon, both completely destroyed. To the south is Candi Bubrah dating from the first state of Candi Sewu: it has a square plan but underwent changes similar to those on the main temple and which were very carefully executed. Candi Lumbung, in the same direction as Candi Bubrah but further south, was probably built after the adoption of the cruciform plan about 790, but before the modification of the doors took place. The stairways and door-frames of these supplementary temples were added. The cruciform plan is shown by markedly projecting niches in the south, west and north facades of the central sanctuary. These were designed to be open but, notwithstanding the difficulty, a door-frame was inserted, though this is only visible on the south side.

Candi Sajiwan, in the village of the same name near the Prambanan racecourse, was probably constructed after 790 on a cruciform plan containing a square cella. The entrance was transformed as in Candi Sewu.

These two important architectural movements, that is, the transformation from a square to a cruciform plan and the modification of the entrances, occurred at the same time as the extension of Buddhism, at the expense of Hinduism, northwards to the upper reaches of the Progo River. The architectural consequences of this event affected Candi Borobudur (Colour Plate 5), the name of which is a contraction of an expression meaning, as de Casparis has established, 'Mountain of accumulation of merits of the ten states of Bodhisattva'.

5　Borobudur, north side

The decline of Hinduism had left a stepped pyramid which was far from complete. Only the first and second terraces were finished but the walls were bare and the outlines of the building were uncarved (Plate 5). This huge stone mass could have been abandoned, for it was difficult to adapt to Buddhism. However, leaving in evidence such an obvious manifestation of Hinduism was probably not judged politically prudent, and the work was taken up again, most likely just after 790, adapting as best as possible the forms and the iconography already introduced at Candi Sewu. However, the size of the worksite, made more difficult by partial collapses, did not allow the second state of the monument to be completed before the approaches were changed, and causing a third stage in its development. This change was possibly introduced while work was still continuing, without any interruption, and caused some parts already finished to be taken up again and some reliefs already completed to be obliterated.

Candi Borobudur is associated with the two other temples built on the same east-west axis, Candi Pawon and Candi Mendut. Both are raised on remains of brick shrines, aligned with a fourth on the remains of which nothing has been rebuilt, located in the cemetery of Bajong village, between Mendut and Pawon.

Candi Mendut has a square plan and rests on a very high foundation up which one climbs by a stairway with a low balustrade decorated with reliefs. The cella is occupied by three large statues. In the centre is the Cakyamuni Buddha preaching the sermon at Benares, on his left is Lokesvara, the Bodhisattva who refused to become a Buddha as long as all men on earth were not saved, and to his right is a Bodhisattva whose identity has not been clearly established. The porch at Candi Mendut was changed several times and a restoration of the first state is not possible, though it was lower than the present one and there was an opening through which the morning sun lit up the face of Cakyamuni.

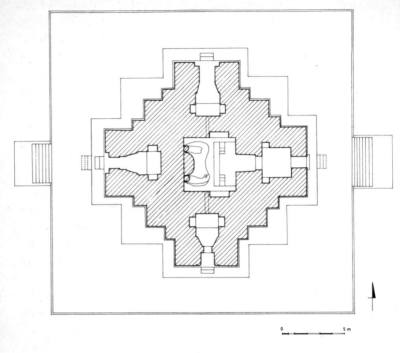

Figure 6. Wat Keo (Chaiya, Thailand), plan

Candi Pawon is also on a square plan, with a porch. The whole appears to have been built without changes, but the restoration in comparatively recent times was radical and one cannot be sure what the original form was like.

It can be seen from these comments that Buddhist architecture in these fifty-five years is perfectly coherent, following broad movements which modified the construction of monuments, and leads to the scheme below:

	Work programmes beginning in 775	Work programmes beginning in 790	Work changing the approaches
South central Java	Kalasan I Sewu I	Kalasan II Sewu II Lumbung I Sajiwan I	Kalasan III Sewu III Lumbung II Sajiwan II
North central Java		Borobudur II Mendut II	Borobudur III Mendut III

Note: Candi Mendut and Candi Borobudur in their first states were probably Hindu foundations (see Chapter 1).

Buddhism created architectural models that allowed devotees to practise their religious rites. Complex architectural forms were not therefore disseminated, but types of buildings were developed which allowed these rites to be carried out. The plan of the shrine at Paharpur in Bangladesh (the Somapura Vihara, for example, built in the very last years of the eighth century), is comparable but not identical to the plan of Candi Kalasan or Candi Sewu after their last transformations. The diffusion of this plan, on very different scales, can be seen in Pagan in Burma or in the south of Thailand at Chaiya (Wat Keo, for example, Figure 6, dating from the tenth century).

The plan of Borobudur, as it was taken over by the Buddhists from its Hindu origins, is in the form of a type of stupa established in the first centuries of the Christian era in Bengal, where the extremely ruined stupa at Nandangarh had a diameter of more than 100 metres. This model continued to be used in Burma. To see what Borobudur looked like at the time of its second transformation, one should study the Schewezigon and the Mingalazedi temples of the twelfth and thirteenth centuries in Pagan.

3

Wooden Temples of the Eighth and Ninth Centuries

THE wooden constructions of the eighth and ninth centuries have entirely disappeared and the architectural elements shown in the reliefs at Borobudur and Prambanan provide the only sources of information about them. The architectural models imported from the south of India were essentially wooden buildings which gradually were transposed into more durable materials. Sometimes an aspect of the models which has completely disappeared in India can be found in these reliefs.

This is true of wooden Pallava temples which can only with difficulty be reconstituted from Indian models, but the task is facilitated with the help of details in the reliefs at Borobudur. For example, one of the reliefs on the third gallery, south side (Figure 7) shows a temple where the upright structures are placed completely outside the building on a masonry base (Figure 8). This is expressed in India in stone, in the Shore Temple of Mahabalipuram near Madras, by the projection in relief, on the outer wall of the temple, of pillars resting on upright lions. These same animals, completely detached from the main structure, can be found on a relief at Borobudur on the lower level of the first gallery, east side. A recent discovery in the south of Thailand shows the same upright lions carved in the round in limestone, completely independent of the masonry as in the examples just cited and incomprehensible without them. This type of shrine consisted of a narrow gallery placed between pillars bearing the roof timbers and the wall of the main building. Inside, it would seem that four substantial pillars, on which the structure of the false storeys was built, took up a good deal of space in the cella.

0   20 cm

Figure 7. Borobudur, building shown on a relief, third gallery, south side

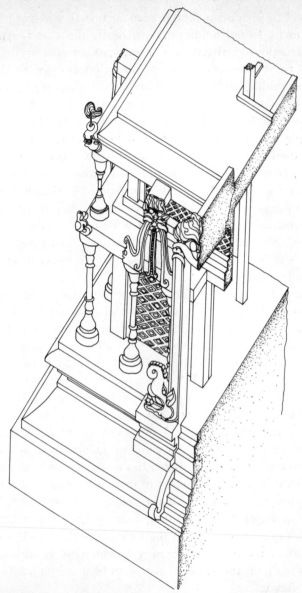

Figure 8. Tentative reconstruction of the building shown in Figure 7

The relief of a wooden temple seen in Figure 2 shows the origin of many stone buildings, particularly those at Dieng. This construction consisted of a framework of roof timbers resting on pillars grouped in fours, doubtless because of the difficulty in finding individual pillars of sufficient girth, but with the difference from the previous example in that the pillars were entirely incorporated into the structure. However, the principle remains the same; the matting forming the partitions, still used in the same way in traditional Central Javanese homes, was placed on the inside and sometimes in the foundation which was originally entirely constructed in wood: there were small pilasters in the recesses of the foundation separating the horizontal mouldings and this left empty spaces which were closed with matting. There are many illustrations of these details at Borobudur; for example, on the lower level of the first gallery, west side.

The main sanctuaries of Candi Plaosan and Candi Sari are a translation into stone of a wooden model of which many examples can be seen at Borobudur (Figure 9) and at Prambanan (Figure 10). The latter shows a building divided into three cellas on two storeys and at Plaosan a loft can be seen between the upper level and the roof; the roof rests on beams where the ridge is held by the weight of the outward-inclining gables. This technique is very old, and was imported into Indonesia in the Bronze Age, in the wake of the Dong-Son civilization. In the National Museum in Jakarta is a bronze drum discovered in Sumatra which has engraved on it shapes of houses of this style, and there are many examples at Borobudur (Figure 11). On some of the reliefs at Prambanan, in particular on panel X of the balustrade of the Siva temple (see Figure 12 and Figure 13 for the location of the panel), can be seen part of the detail of the way beams were assembled; some are shown on the same section with both a longitudinal and a side facade.

0   20 cm

Figure 9. Borobudur, building shown on a relief, first gallery, south side

Figure 10. Prambanan, building shown on a relief, east balustrade of Candi Brahma

This technique of the ridge in tension was widespread not only throughout Java and the Batak area of Sumatra but also in the Toraja lands of Sulawesi. Probably because of the increasing scarcity of large straight tree trunks in the Indonesian forests, the technique ceased to be used for big buildings. The appearance of the structures was maintained by using different beam methods. Shorter beams stabilized the deformations due to the tension of the roof ridge. The sagging roofline, due to the weight of the rafters, is characteristic of these buildings, and it was kept for no other reason than tradition. However, the technique was maintained for small constructions, especially for granaries, because it allowed the utilization of the whole volume of the roofing which was not encumbered with trusses; a granary of this type had already appeared in a Borobudur relief (first gallery, north side, lower level). Buildings of this type persisted until the fourteenth century in Java (some can still be seen in Sulawesi), where they were dedicated to Sri, the wife of Visnu and the protectress of rice. In the region of Porong in East Java, a carving in brick or stone showing a sagging roofline, in no specific architectural context, as at Candi Pari or Candi Belahan, for example, is sufficient to indicate the cult of Visnu.

It is difficult to determine what materials were used for the roofing. Most likely thatch or palm leaves were used, together with terracotta elements for the roof ridge and the hips. Nevertheless, several buildings on the reliefs of the balustrades of the temples at Prambanan can be seen covered with wood shingles or flat rectangular terracotta tiles. One of them, on the west balustrade of the Visnu temple, is covered with very broad tiles, in all probability made of terracotta, with a very indented lower edge. This particular type of tile continued to be used up to the fourteenth century, when the use of ceramic pieces for roofing became general. It was only towards the fifteenth century, in all likelihood, that the tiles

0   20 cm

Figure 11. Borobudur, building shown on a relief, balustrade of the first gallery, west side

10 cm

0

Figure 12. Prambanan, building shown on a relief, balustrade of Candi Siva (panel X)

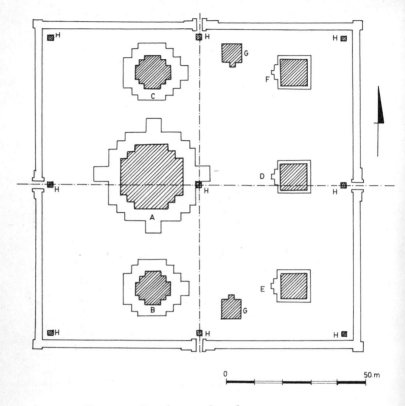

Figure 13. Prambanan, plan of upper terrace

A   Candi Siva
B   Candi Brahma
C   Candi Visnu
D   Candi Nandin
E   Candi Hamsa
F   Candi Garuda
G   Candi Apit
H   Shrines for the laying-out points

of Chinese origin, looking like a horizontally laid S, were introduced and which are still frequently used for roofing in Java today.

The reliefs show that the wooden temples had extremely varied architectural forms and that, in spite of a lack of technical flexibility, the builders of the eighth and ninth centuries were in complete mastery of wood as a construction material. This is probably the reason for the transposition of forms suitable to roof timbers into stone and brick, the use of which was not so well understood. This transposition into another material did not allow for the emergence of new forms adapted to materials which made the buildings last longer.

4

The Hindu Renaissance after 832

WHEN the Hindu dynasty of Sanjaya reunified Central Java after 832, there appeared at the same time a new cultural impetus from India. In architecture, this is shown in new rites for the laying out of buildings and in new methods of construction. This renaissance led to huge architectural ensembles, the biggest of which is Candi Prambanan, built on the east bank of the Opak River, near Candi Sewu. The site was not chosen at random. By building near the main Sailendra sanctuary and without destroying it, the conquerors confirmed their authority and their tolerance. The same political overtones are relevant with the location on the west bank of the Progo River, not far from Borobudur, of the triple sanctuary of Candi Banon. The temple has not survived but the three statues of Siva, Visnu and Brahma from the temple are to be found in the National Museum in Jakarta.

Candi Prambanan (Plate 6) dedicated to the cult of Siva, is built on three different levels corresponding to the three precincts. The outer wall has been almost entirely destroyed (though the south gate of this precinct is still to be seen against the northern wall of the modern theatre). It was built with a different orientation from the two inner precinct walls which were laid out according to the cardinal points, with the principal side facing east (Plate 7). None of the buildings constructed between the outer wall and the second enclosure has survived. In the western part, as the previously mentioned inscription of 856 indicated, the Opak River was diverted for the benefit of the temple. This was accompanied by major irrigation works upstream. Between the second enclosure and the inner wall, the space was divided into three tiers

6   Prambanan, Candi Siva

7   Prambanan, Candi Siva, east entrance

which altogether housed 224 small shrines, the Candi Perwara ('perwara' means 'bridesmaid'), consisting of a cella laid out following the cardinal points. The corner shrines have two openings facing each of the possible directions. So the corner shrine of the upper level, reconstructed in the south-east corner, opens to both the south and the east. The upper part of the Candi Perwara consists of three false storeys and a finial. Each of the horizontal levels formed by the false storeys supports structures of reduced size. The inner wall (Figure 13) encloses the main shrines of Candi Siva in the centre, Candi Visnu to the north and Candi Brahma to the south. These three temples face east; in front of each is a temple dedicated to the mount of the gods, the bull Nandin for Siva, the fabulous bird Garuda for Visnu and the sacred goose Hamsa for Brahma. Of these three animals, only the magnificent bull is still in place. Some doubt arises about the identification of the other two, for which different gods could have been substituted.

On this terrace can still be seen, to the north and south, the two Candi Apit ('apit' means 'squashed' or 'pinched'). These temples have the same features as the three main temples but are on a narrower plan, hence their name. Also found here are the nine small shrines housing the location of the marker stones which served to trace the alignment that allowed the different constructions to be set up. The central marker is placed under the shrine to the left of the east stairway of Candi Siva and so does not mark the exact spot. The other similar edifices placed on either side of the temple stairways are massive.

The different buildings at Prambanan (with the exception of the small shrines for the marker stones), are of cruciform plan, but only in Candi Siva does this composition take on a structural reality and only this building has four cellas and a connecting corridor to reach the centre. In the cellas the usual iconography is found (Siva in the centre, Agastya on his right,

his son Ganesha behind him and his wife Durga to his left);
however, in the centre, instead of a linga to express the creative
force of the god, is a statue showing the full form of the god. It
may be that this image represents a dead king whose presence
on earth would only have been, in a sense, a reincarnation of
Siva. Around the foundation mass a high balustrade was built
and the inner side is decorated with reliefs depicting the
Ramayana epic. The story begins from the east side, and continues on the south, keeping the monument to one's right.

These are the main scenes (the location of the panels is
shown in Figure 14):

Panel 1: The awakening of the god Visnu in the presence of
his mount, the mythical bird Garuda.

Panel 4: Rama and his brother Laksmana fighting the demons
Subahu and Marica.

Panel 5: The competition to win the hand of Sita, in which
Rama takes part.

Panel 7: The departure of Rama, Laksmana and Sita to exile in
the forest.

Panel 10: Rama fighting the Viradha demons.

Panel 12: Laksmana rejects the advances of the demon
Curpankha transformed into a young maiden; on the same
panel, Rama chases the golden deer, unaware that this is no
other than the demon Marica.

Panel 13: The abduction of Sita by Ravana; on the same panel,
the bird Jatayu receives Sita's ring which it gives to Rama.

Panel 15: Rama meets Hanuman.

Panel 18: The fight between Valin and Rama's ally Surgriva;
Rama intervenes in the fight and kills Valin with an arrow.

Panel 20: Hanuman sees Sita in the palace of Ravana.

Panel 21: Hanuman is made prisoner; on the same panel, he
escapes and sets fire to Ravana's palace with his burning tail.

Panel 24: The building of the dyke to allow Lanka, where
Ravana lives, to be reached.

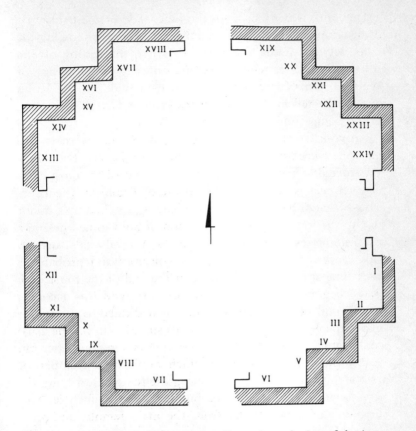

Figure 14. Prambanan, Candi Siva, location and numbering of the inner panels of the balustrade

The story is continued on the inner side of the balustrade of the temple dedicated to Brahma, to the south, showing the fights between Rama and Ravana's army, the freeing of Sita and the life of the reunited couple reigning over the city of Ayodhya. On the inner side of the balustrade on the Visnu temple, the reliefs illustrate an account of Krisna's exploits, Krisna being another incarnation of Visnu.

Around AD 850 many Hindu establishments were started but none were as important as Candi Prambanan. They were constructed in brick as well as in stone. One of the most complete temples is located in the village of Sambisari (hence its name of Candi Sambisari: Colour Plate 7), reached by a minor road to the left going in the direction of Solo some one and a half kilometres after the turn-off to Yogyakarta's airport. This sanctuary was covered with volcanic sand probably a short time after it was plundered at the end of the fourteenth or the beginning of the fifteenth century, and this accounts for its good state of preservation. It is dedicated to the cult of Siva in the form of a linga placed on a superb plinth. The usual iconography is found in the external niches. On the terrace can be seen the bases of the pillars which would have been part of a wooden pavilion entirely covering the temple, justifying the very squat proportions of the building. Three small terraces surrounded by balustrades front the main temple, and were probably decorated with statues or linga in the open air. The method of laying out is the same as in Prambanan and the marker stones were replaced in a similar fashion by small linga, of which many are still in place. The central linga is missing but the hollow for its base on the plinth, to the right of the staircase of the main sanctuary, can be seen. This ensemble is surrounded by a precinct wall make of volcanic tuff which has openings on the axes of the four sides. The foundation, also of tuff, has not been completely excavated because of a rise in the underground water level. It was in the form of a stepped pyramid with stairways projecting from the axes, the same as the first state of Borobudur, but on a smaller scale.

This very large construction programme of relatively small Hindu temples (the most accessible being the three Candi Kuning on the road from Blabak to Boyolali, Candi Sari Sorogedug and Candi Idjo on the Ratu Boko plateau, and Candi Merak near Klaten), was accompanied by a rehabilitation of older shrines, adapting them to contemporary fashion. This is seen at Dieng with the construction of new precincts and also in a temple as far away from Central Java as Candi Badut (see Chapter 1). The adaptation of this temple was wholesale; most probably the complete ritual of laying out was changed by removing the marker stones and above all by making the precinct excentric. The decoration was partially changed by transforming the upper parts of the monsters' heads at the top of the niches into a temple on which gods scatter flowers, similar to the decoration in Prambanan.

Although the Sanjaya were themselves Hindu, they ruled in the south of Central Java over a Buddhist majority, for whom they, in a manner of speaking, reappropriated the most important monuments built by the Sailendra. This is especially evident at Borobudur, where the doorways giving access to the first gallery were reconstructed using a technique similar to that used at Prambanan. The foundation was also modified by extending it to the edge of the paving, leaving only the space for a narrow gutter. A remodelling of the doorway using the same technique can also be seen at Candi Mendut. In Candi Sewu a renewal of the statuary was begun and left unfinished.

Above all, the Sanjaya built major new Buddhist foundations, Candi Sari and Candi Plaosan. These two monuments have a similar plan, reproducing wooden sanctuaries of an antique model (similar ones can be seen on the reliefs at Borobudur). The first to be built was probably Candi Sari, located near Candi Kalasan but on the other side of the road

to Solo. The six cellas of this shrine are arranged in two levels
and the upper floor was reached by a wooden stairway. The
first step in stone remains and served for the start of the string-
board which held the staircase. This building is especially
remarkable for its very fine external decoration consisting of
female divinities (Colour Plate 8) and Bodhisattvas playing
musical instruments.

The outer wall and all the additional buildings around
Candi Sari have completely disappeared. Their layout can be
envisaged thanks to Candi Plaosan (Colour Plate 9), about
two kilometres east of Candi Sewu. An inscription discovered
on the site relates details of its foundation: it says that in the
courtyard of an old temple built on the same site, but almost
in ruins, appeared a magnificent Buddha statue. This super-
natural event was interpreted by the Buddhist priests as
expressing the desire of the Buddha to see a new shrine constructed on the same spot. From this pious legend one need
only retain the fact that another shrine existed before the
present temple. The remains of the earlier building were, in
fact, found when the southern temple was being restored,
merged in the foundation of the later shrine.

Candi Plaosan faces west and consists of a double sanctuary
(the southern one has been restored and the northern one is
currently being restored). Each has the same layout as Candi
Sari and comprises six cellas. The iconography of the lower
cellas can be reconstructed: it consisted of two Bodhisattvas
on either side of a Buddha statue which has disappeared. It is
possible that the scene was similar to that at Candi Mendut.
Nothing remains of the upper flooring. It is likely, given the
location of the windows, that there was only one statue. The
two main buildings are surrounded by a wall and 174 smaller
constructions of two different types—58 shrines and 116
stupas. These are distributed in three concentric rows and are
endowments to the temple made by officials of the kingdom

who had their titles carved on their gifts (these inscriptions can be seen on the upper band of the foundation of the shrines in the north-west corner of the first row).

This considerable building effort over such a short period of less than seventy years caused a return to simple constructions in which wood played a more important part. The early examples of this reversion can be seen on the Ratu Boko plateau, two kilometres south of Prambanan, in the group known as the Kraton, meaning 'palace'. The buildings were constructed for purposes which are still not entirely clear, but several Sanskrit inscriptions, dating from the end of the ninth century, have been discovered on the site. Three refer to Sivaism and another fragment relates to Buddhism with a possible reference to a famous Cingalese monastery. All these epigraphic remains are of a religious nature and it is likely, therefore, that at least a major part of the buildings served a religious purpose.

The group was enclosed by a wall with an entrance in the form of a triple porch built on two different levels (Plate 8); it was restored in the 1930s by Dutch archaeologists. It was built in stone, including the roofing, but this, instead of resting on stone corbels as in earlier temples, was built on a solid wooden structure which those responsible for the restoration replaced with reinforced concrete. Inside the surrounding wall are several terraces on which wooden pavilions were most likely constructed. The terrace, called the Istana ('istana' also means 'palace'), on the south-east of the plateau, is surrounded by a wall with three entrances; the southern wall next to a rock face has no opening. This enclosure is built in two parts; the base as usual is andesite and the upper part of very poor quality white volcanic tuff which is, however, extremely easy to work. The terrace proper was built with care, particularly in respect of the paving stones, made of large blocks of andesite. Rain water was led away from the base of the surrounding wall

through fine gargoyles.

On a lower level, to the south of the Istana, are two enclosures called the Chinese gardens. Only the approaches and a small part of the surrounding walls remain of these buildings, but the detail on their outlines is remarkably fine. From this period, that is the end of the ninth century, the use of volcanic tuff became more general and a huge quarry to the south-west of the Ratu Boko plateau can still clearly be seen. Because of the fragility of tuff, few important buildings remain which were constructed in it; however, the Payak bathing place, eleven kilometres from Yogyakarta on the Wonosari road, is one.

The scale of such construction over some seventy years inevitably produced a reaction and led to a slowing down in the creation of large religious buildings. Furthermore, the shift to a less durable though more easily worked material, as well as the use of different methods of construction (using wood to uphold stone, as in later buildings in Angkor), not only reduced the number of buildings which have survived from this later period, but those which have endured are also of indifferent quality.

5

The Architecture of the Tenth
and Eleventh Centuries

THIS long period corresponds historically to the transfer of power from the centre of Java to the east and the existence of the so-called kingdom of Kediri (1050-1221). The architectural remains of the period are few and when archaeological excavation brings buildings to light, they are of little importance (as in Gurah, near Kediri). A lack of physical means can also be observed in the use of older temples (in Candi Badut, for example; see Chapter 1) or in contemporary buildings being periodically altered according to changing needs, fashions and rituals.

During this period, bathing places were built. This type of construction had existed for a long time, above all as very simple canalizations of mountain streams, as is seen in reliefs (for example, the twelfth panel of the balustrade in Candi Siva at Prambanan), but was greatly extended. The use of these structures is not easy to determine. The *Negarakertagama*, the Javanese fourteenth century text, makes two allusions to their use, firstly in describing the ritual bath of the king (Song 19, Verse 2), and then in briefly touching on the eroticism of certain ceremonies celebrated in these pools (Song 27, Verse 1). This second use is sometimes confirmed by the names given to the constructions, since one of them is called 'Kasurangganan' which Kern translates as 'the nymphs' bower'.

At Jalatunda (located near Trawas in the Modjokerto region), a bathing place dating from 977 was constructed (Plate 9) and comprises three elements assembled in the same ornamental pool; two tanks for the ablutions proper, sur-

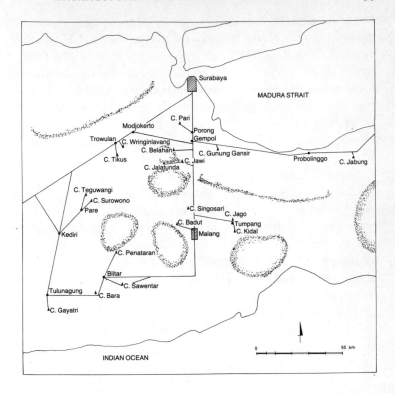

Figure 15. Map of East Java

rounding a central mass (Figure 16) supporting a representation of Mount Meru (now found in the National Museum in
Jakarta). This had five spouts producing water taken from a
nearby spring on Mount Penungunggan. In the fourteenth
century this installation was largely transformed by the addi-
tion of reliefs illustrating the Arjuna saga. At the time of the
excavation of the building in the middle of the nineteenth
century, an urn was discovered containing ashes and some
fragments of gold leaf.

Some of these establishments eventually took on a funerary
function, as is seen in the Belahan bathing place (Belahan is
reached by a small track branching off from the road from
Surabaya to Malang, two kilometres from Gempol going in
the direction of Malang). A chronogram, or inscription
including the date, indicates that in 1049 the monument probably received the ashes of King Airlanga. This bathing place
in its present state only has a single pool fed by two fountains
in the form of female divinities, Laksmi and Sri, the two wives
of Visnu (Plate 10). The iconography was completed by a very
beautiful statue of Visnu on a Garuda, currently found in the
Modjokerto museum.

At the end of the tenth century, the Balinese prince Udayana
married a princess of the reigning dynasty in East Java; this
marriage was probably the consequence of a certain increase
of Javanese influence in Bali. This is shown by the adoption
of several rituals and customs and by the construction of some
monuments which look rather Javanese. These buildings are
grouped in the Gianyar district of Bali: at the beginning of
the eleventh century near the village of Bedulu, the bathing
place of Gua Gajah (the elephant cave) was built. Like those
in Java it has three main elements: two tanks separated by a
now destroyed central motif which, however, was not as big
as at Jalatunda. The water came, as in Belahan, from statues

1 Gedong Songo, group III

2 Gedong Songo, group VI

3 Candi Kalasan, east facade

4 Candi Borobudur, relief, third gallery, north side

5 Candi Borobudur, north façade

6 Candi Sewu, south facade of the main shrine

7 Candi Sambisari, general view

8 Candi Sari, relief on the east facade

9 Candi Plaosan, southern shrine, south-east corner

10 Statue of Ganesha from Candi Bara

11 Candi Jawi, north-east corner

12 Candi Jabung, south facade

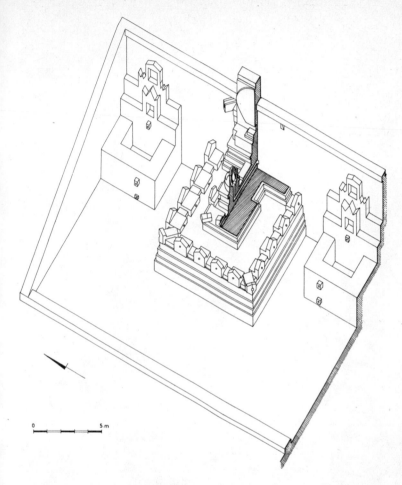

Figure 16. The bathing place at Jalatunda, schematic restoration

9 Jalatunda general view

which here represented divinities carrying an urn from which the water flowed.

The tombs of Gunung Kawi (the mountain of poems) (Plate 11), near the village of Tampaksiring in Bali, were established towards the end of the eleventh century and probably contained the ashes of King Anak Wungsu (1049-1077) and his wives who burned themselves on the royal pyre. These nine tombs cut in the rock are in the shape of a temple and constitute the oldest traces of the style of architecture which was to have such success in the following centuries in Java. The reliefs all reproduce the same construction, consisting of the central body supporting three false storeys decorated with miniature temples.

The base of Candi Jago (the cock temple) in the village of Tumpang, constructed at the end of the thirteenth century, is decorated with reliefs comprising numerous views of buildings that establish the state of architecture as it existed at the turn of the twelfth century. A certain lapse of time was needed for the forms to be sufficiently widespread to be employed as decoration in reliefs. Among the constructions shown can be seen many where the roof is in tiers (for example, the northeast corner of the lower part of the base) and resting on square corbels; this was probably done by using radiating rafters (Figure 18). This type of structure came from southern India but was used in Java and Bali with very different beamwork techniques from those in India. The possibilities of the new beamwork technique are numerous but they were only used, at first, to cover two types of structures: the small square pavilions with the roofing upheld by four pillars (later these roof coverings sometimes have only one central pillar forming a sort of enormous mushroom), and structures with tiered roofs with the same principles of composition as the reliefs at Gunung Kawi, each level being slightly smaller in base than that immediately below and of diminishing height. These

10   Belahan, Laksmi

11   Gunung Kawi, carved temple in the main group

structures are at the origin of the Balinese meru and probably looked very similar to them.

In spite of the lack of important buildings, this period was rich in architectural discoveries which were only to be fully exploited in the subsequent centuries.

6

The Temples of
the Singosari Kings

THE temples constructed during the reign of the Singosari dynasty (1222-1293) can be divided into two types, those on the one hand built like Candi Kidal (Figure 17), and on the other those like Candi Jago. This is a very summary division because it necessarily eliminates the now completely destroyed wooden temples, which must have been very numerous. The proof of these is seen in the reliefs of monuments, and also in the existence of some isolated statues. For example, the superb stone Ganesha of Candi Bara (in the village of Tuliskaiyo near Blitar) which dates from 1239, is probably all that remains of a very important wooden shrine needed to shelter such a large statue (Colour Plate 10).

Candi Kidal, located in the village of Rejokidal near Tumpang, was built around 1260. It comprises two main elements: the sanctuary proper and a small terrace on which there were probably two or three wooden pavilions. A relief on the north facade of Candi Jawi reproduces one of these terraces with three pavilions. These constructions were enclosed by a surrounding wall which opened on the four cardinal points, but none of the entrances has survived. The sanctuary (Plate 12) consists of a single square cella for a now disappeared statue. Externally the monument was divided into three parts: the base, the body of the building, and the tower above it. The tower is hollow and the chamber constituting the internal space has no opening. Even though the internal masonry was carefully arranged, this chamber was probably simply a way of reducing the weight of the structure, avoiding excessive pressure on the corbelling covering the cella. The base is decorated on three

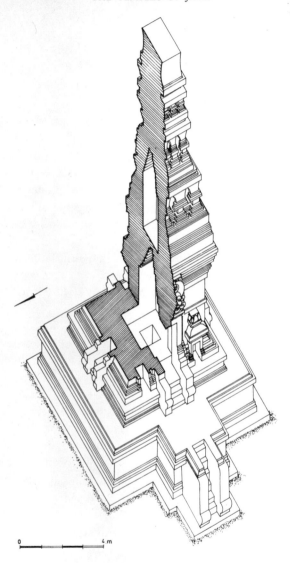

Figure 17. Schematic restoration of a temple of the same type as Candi Kidal

sides with reliefs. On the north Garuda is shown carrying a feminine divinity, probably Sri, the wife of Visnu, born from the churning of the sea of milk; to the east Garuda is seen bearing a container holding the essence of immortality; and to the south can be seen the serpent which doubtless took part in the churning of the sea of milk. On the west side of the base is a stairway giving access to the cella. The body of the building is on a square plan with a projecting element on each of the four sides suggesting, however, a cruciform plan (this is expressed in its entirety in Candi Singosari in the village of the same name). The niches on the north, east and south facades are treated as true doorways to the cella, each with a small stairway in front, with the first step placed above the upper level of the base. On the west side, the doorway giving access to the cella is surrounded by two niches flush with the base and which would have contained statues for the guardian.

The masonry course marks the start of a second false storey and the tower above it is in ruins. The proportions of the whole and the numerous stones not utilized during restoration are sufficient for one to be able to imagine the entire size of the original tower. It was divided into three false storeys of diminishing height towards the top; each of the three levels had sixteen miniature constructions with their dimensions in proportion to the corresponding storey. This was with the aim of increasing the perspective effect and artificially elongating the monument. The finial consisted of two parts: the lower part was formed by a succession of horizontal mouldings bearing the upper part, consisting of just one plain or barely decorated section, probably square, though it could unusually have been circular.

Very few temples like this remain from this period, since the great height of the towers, usually around fifteen metres, made them very susceptible to earthquakes. Three main temples have survived. Candi Sawentar (Plate 13), in the village of the same

12   Candi Kidal, west side

13 Candi Sawentar, west side

name near Blitar, was begun at the beginning of the thirteenth century but for some unknown reason was not completed. Candi Singosari (Plate 14) was built in the capital a little before it was partially destroyed in 1292; the temple was spared because in 1359 King Hayam Wuruk of the Majapahit dynasty came to the shrine to pay homage to his deified ancestors. Lastly, Candi Jawi (Colour Plate 11) in the village of Candiwates near Prigen, was probably built by King Kertanagara (1268-1292). It houses a statue showing Siva on one side and the Buddha Aksobhya (see Chapter 1) on the other half, expressing in this way King Kertanagara's belief in the profound unity of Sivaism and Buddhism. It seems likely that the statue was considered as a funerary monument to the king who ordered its construction; in the *Negarakertagama*, Verses 73 and 74, the temple is mentioned as being his tomb. If architecturally Candi Jawi is the same type as Candi Kidal, there are differences and the co-existence of the two religions is shown in these. The foundation, with carved reliefs, is Sivaite and the finial in the form of a stupa is Buddhist. Candi Jawi is, moreover, one of the most complete temples of this period. It still has moats all around the shrine, which makes it unique today, but these must have been common in the thirteenth century. It also has the remains of a double enclosure, and the base of the internal western pavilion giving access to the two enclosures also remains. This building is no longer in its original state, having been considerably transformed in the fourteenth century. The entrance pavilion from the outside was on the north side and the corners of the enclosure were marked by blocks of masonry with some decoration. This plan, with numerous variations, served as the model of several Balinese temples, for example, that at Pura Taman Ajun of the seventeenth century, located in Mengwi in Badung district.

Temples of the type of Candi Jago are of the same form as those of Candi Kidal, but are built on a very high base divided

14   Candi Singosari, east side

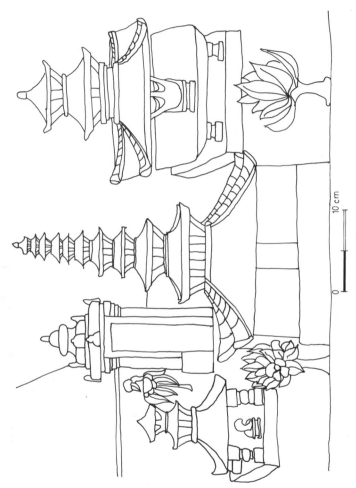

Figure 18. Candi Jago, building shown on the second level of the foundation, east side

10 cm

0

into three levels. The temples are not completely centred on the base, and are often markedly displaced to the east.

Candi Jago (Figure 18) was built around 1280 and faces west. The shrine consisted of a single square cella in which the plinth for the statue was located; it was displaced subsequently and is now to be found lying against the base of the monument, in the west side. The iconography was Buddhist, and the main statue was probably that of Amaghapaca, also to be found in the temple courtyard. To the right and left were statues of the Bodhisattva Sudhana and the goddess Cyamatara which are now in the National Museum in Jakarta. The rites practised in the cella included the lustration of the main statue and water used in the ceremony was collected in the basin formed by the rim of the plinth. The water was then removed through two gargoyles carved in relief on the sides of the plinth (showing in this way by how much the original volume of the stone was reduced), and was collected in two small wells hollowed into the cella paving. The two stairways cutting across the base had three flights, one for each level. The lower four faced west but the upper two are perpendicular, facing north and south and ending at a landing just before the cella. The main interest of Candi Jago is its four rows of reliefs; although their meaning is still somewhat obscure, they are extremely rich in details relating to thirteenth century Javanese life.

This temple underwent major renovation in 1343 and from this date its plan had much influence until the end of the four-teenth century. In particular, three temples of this type were built during the Majapahit period and, by and large, kept close to the traditional architecture of the thirteenth century. Candi Jabung (Colour Plate 12), in the village of the same name near Probolingo, was completed in 1354. It was built of brick and externally has a circular plan though the inside of the cella is square. It was conceived as a Buddhist shrine, probably the funerary temple of a princess of the Majapahit dynasty. Its finial

15   Candi Teguwangi, south-east corner

is partly ruined but was probably in the form of a stupa. Candi Teguwangi (Plate 15), in the village of the same name near Pare in the Kediri region, was probably started around 1370 but was not completed, though the reliefs decorating the south side of the first level of the base were finished. Candi Surowono, in the village of Canggu not far from Candi Teguwangi, was built around 1390 and the reliefs on the first level of the base illustrate several texts, the *Arjunawiwaha*, the *Bubuksa-Gagak-Aking* and the *Sri Tanjung*. However, the distribution of the illustrations does not follow these three texts in order but a plan related to the monument, so on the north-east corner are scenes relating to asceticism, and on the south-east corner are those relating to royalty.

The builders of the thirteenth century, therefore, while remaining very close to the architecture of earlier centuries—Candi Sembrodo in Dieng has the same plan as Candi Singosari—entirely altered the appearance of the Hindu and Buddhist temples and the decoration became more explicitly symbolic.

7

The Temples of
the Majapahit Kings

NUMEROUS temples were built during the Majapahit period
(1293–c.1530). The master builders often followed the two
architectural types established in the preceding period, but they
also created their own models. Contemporary literary sources
allow us to see how the architecture was conceived and viewed.
In Th. Pigeaud's literal translation, here is a passage from the
Negarakertagama (Song 37, Verses 1 and 2):

To be described are the arrangements of that eminent religious
domain there, its ornaments unparalleled. A doorway utterly splendid
with a girdle in the forecourt, the height thereof unmeasured. In the
inside its yard is terraced, orderly placed are the houses beautiful, at its
sides. Crowded are all kinds of flower-trees for offerings. . . . A
temple tower has its place in the centre, showing something to
be wondered at: the imposing appearance thereof, holy, high,
of the aspect of the mountain Meru. A Shiwa-abode, in Shiwa's
likeness, has its place in the interior. . . .

It can be seen from this description of a Sivaite shrine that
the entrance doorway had become an essential element, and its
great height was enhanced further by perspective effects. Unfortunately, few of these constructions have survived; the only one
which is almost complete but is of fairly modest proportions is
Candi Bajang Ratu (located near Trowulan not far from Candi
Tikus: Plate 16). It was probably constructed in the first half of
the fourteenth century and is decorated with rather eroded
reliefs around its base illustrating the narrative of Sri Tanjung.
Higher on the decorative elements marking the start of the
enclosure wall are carved scenes taken from the Ramayana. This
doorway led to a monument which has now disappeared.

16 Candi Bajang Ratu

Most of the ruined entrances to temples can be reconstructed thanks to this example; for example, Candi Jawi in its final state or Candi Wringin Lawang (meaning the shrine of the fig doorway, located near Trowulan). After crossing the doorway, one came into a courtyard with several wooden buildings; the reliefs at Candi Jago (for example, on the second level on the east side) show the complete arrangement. Inside the walls there were very many buildings, for the most part consisting of a simple four-sided roof, upheld by four pillars resting on a foundation. Sometimes these constructions were more elaborate; a carved example is found on the relief of the main terrace at Penataran, on the first level of the west side (Figure 19: Penataran is to the north of Blitar). This has a double foundation; first of all, there is a fairly ill-defined masonry structure on the ground supporting the four bases of the pillars, then a small two-stepped rise. Above the bases, the horizontal beams upheld the joists supporting the floor forming the second foundation. Above this there were the four richly decorated pillars. The roof was composed of three superimposed elements covered with tiles; the beamwork was probably radiating. When the roof builders set about creating a mosque at the end of the fifteenth century, they were unable to conceive new techniques more suited to their purpose. So the Javanese wooden mosque is covered with a combination of several superimposed spreading beam arrangements.

This type of structure was not just used for the adjacent buildings but also for temples, as for example with Candi Gayatri (in the village of Boyolangu near Tulunagun). This is a Buddhist shrine built on two superimposed brick foundations supporting the stone pillar bases. Two of these are dated to the equivalent of 1369 and 1389, doubtless indicating the consecration and a rebuilding of the structure. This is seen at the base where two walls decorated with mouldings are visible, one in front of the other. The temple proper consisted of two concen-

Figure 19. Penataran, building shown on a relief on the lower level of the west side of the main temple

tric rows of pillars marking out a square space, in the middle of
which was placed a statue of a goddess, probably Prajnapara-
mita, which is today very mutilated. Following the description
in the *Negarakertagama*, around these buildings can be found
flowering trees and the centre of the main shrine is explicitly
designed to look like Mount Meru, the dwelling of the gods.

The shrine was most often built on the model of Candi
Kidal, although there was great variety in the different structures. At Penataran, the main terrace, built about 1347, does not
show Mount Meru but an aerial palace (Figure 19), where the
gods reside. The upper level of the terrace was decorated with
lions and winged snakes (Plate 17) which seem to carry the
temple in the air; this is, in fact, similar to Khmer architecture
of the thirteenth century. The reliefs on the lower level of the
same terrace illustrate the Ramayana; the panel of Figure 19
shows Sita in the palace of Ravana. If the series is compared
with those at Candi Siva in Prambanan, it can be seen that the
choice of scenes has only a few points in common: the burning
of Ravana's palace by Hanuman (panel 21 at Candi Siva, and
the east side near the south-west corner at Penataran), or the
construction of the dyke to reach Lanka (panel 24 at Candi Siva
and the two middle panels on the south side at Penataran). This
probably corresponds to a kind of literary evolution and to an
associated interpretation, which is not easy to determine. The
second level is of poorer quality and difficult to make out.
When King Hayam Wuruk visited this temple in 1359 it was far
from finished.

In the same enclosure as the main terrace, many other buildings were constructed: the dated temple (so called because
above the doorway is carved the equivalent date of 1369) is the
same type as Candi Kidal but with markedly more compact
proportions. On the north-west corner of the terrace and a little
lower down, a bathing place was built. Although today it is in a
poor state of preservation, the reliefs remain, showing fables

17 Penataran, main terrace, upper level

18 Penataran, Candi Naga

with animal scenes. To the south of the same terrace, Candi Naga (Plate 18) has been reduced to just its main walls. It seems likely that its roofing was of beamwork and similar to a Balinese meru. To the west, a broad terrace would have had a pavilion (hence the name, the pendopo terrace) and is decorated with a row of reliefs bearing the date equivalent to 1375. Lastly, outside the enclosure, in the village of Penataran proper, is another bathing place; this has been restored and is functioning as it was originally designed. Thanks to these dates, it can be seen that the construction of Penataran took place over the long period, from at least 1347 to 1375, or thirty years for a relatively modest ensemble when compared to Prambanan or Borobudur.

The monuments of the Majapahit capital were for the most part built of brick or wood and because of this have mostly been destroyed. The capital was not really a town but a number of scattered clusters of buildings enclosed by walls, separated by fields and broad open spaces for markets and meetings. What remains of the structures is grouped around Trowulan. Apart from the two doorways of Bajang Ratu and Wringin Lawang already mentioned, the enormous tank Segaran, six hectares in area, can also be seen. The sides of this have been restored and consist of well-faced walls with a landing-stage on the south side. Candi Brahu (Plate 19) has a square plan with projections on its three plain sides. One entered by the now completely collapsed west side, but the corbelling covering the cella remains in place. Candi Minak Jinggo is very ruined and was decorated with carved stone reliefs, now found in the Modjokerto museum. Lastly, Candi Tikus (the mouse shrine, or possibly the shrine of the rat, the mount of Ganesha) is a bathing place with a similar composition as that at Candi Jalatunda (Figure 16), but instead of being on the side of a hill, Candi Tikus is entirely on flat ground. This position did not allow for fountains, although a water pipe went under the

19   Candi Brahu, south side

central mass representing Mount Meru with its five peaks, and the water seemed to flow beneath the mountain.

Candi Pari (in the village of Candipari near Porong: Plate 20) was constructed outside the capital and the date equivalent to 1371 is engraved on the entrance lintel. The temple comprises a vast square cella open to the west and lit by six small windows. The north, south and east facades have a projecting miniature temple of not inconsiderable dimensions. This composition is unusual in Java and may be of foreign derivation, possibly from Champa, but it would seem to be more likely a local innovation such as can be seen partially in nearby monuments, the doorways of Candi Belahan and at Candi Gunung Gansir (in the village of the same name, near Gempol). The master builders of Candi Pari had a broad surface on which to sketch the temple finials and created new forms using perspective effects not only on the vertical plane, but, as at Candi Kidal, also on the horizontal plane. The false storeys can easily take the miniature structures, but they are preceded by three rows of antefixes slightly shifted in their relationship with each other. In this way the depth was artificially increased.

Candi Gunung Gansir (Plate 21) was probably built in the last quarter of the fourteenth century. The structure is in poor condition but it still has a very fine terracotta decoration incorporated in the masonry, showing vases of flowers, imaginary trees covered with fruit and goddesses carrying lotuses. The reliefs above the border of the niches are now scattered around the temple courtyard and reproduce the finials of Candi Pari, with miniature constructions preceded by three rows of antefixes. So that the viewer would fully appreciate the scale of the motif, birds are placed between the reduced structures. From this detail can be seen the great care given by the master builders in regard to the exact perception of the architecture created.

The bathing place of Belahan was considerably modified in

20   Candi Pari, west side

21   Candi Gunung Gansir, east side

the fourteenth century (see Chapter 5). Probably towards 1375 a very long wall, more than 1 000 metres in perimeter, was built, encompassing a vast triangular space. On the north side, the wall is cut by two doorways. The western doorway has in its finial the same composition, on a smaller scale, as at Candi Pari. The eastern doorway has smaller proportions and gave onto a now entirely destroyed temple, though the plinth for a statue remains.

Majapahit architecture shows a unity of conception but also a certain regionalism. With many variations, three schools can be discerned. One centres around the capital, reproducing in brick almost without change the stone architecture of Singosari. A second group around Penataran continues the earlier models in stone but with new forms for the terraces and the architectural sculpture. Lastly, a third group around Candi Pari is no longer content with vertical visual effects but also horizontal ones are introduced. This art had an influence on the architecture of the neighbouring islands. There is no doubt that Balinese temples continue the secondary buildings of the East Javanese shrines such as they are to be seen in the reliefs of Candi Jago, Penataran and Surowono. The brick temples of Muara Jambi in the province of Jambi in Sumatra, or of Padang Lawas in the province of north Sumatra, are partially inspired by Javanese fourteenth century architecture. This influence was felt for a long time and can be seen in Muslim architecture in the roof-lines of many mosques and in entrance doorways, for example, the Magedan gopura of 1536 and the Takolulao gopura of 1574 at Simpang on the island of Madura. Lastly, the rock decoration of the Suniaragi garden at Cirebon, completed in 1741, certainly owes a lot to the similar decoration of Jalatunda and Belahan.

This places the monuments of the fifteenth century in parentheses, as it were. They are numerous but are given over to an often very explicit symbolism which made them entirely un-

22 Candi Ceto, west side

acceptable to Islam. At the beginning of the fifteenth century, Mount Penanggungan (between Belahan and Jalatunda) was entirely rearranged as Mount Meru; its silhouette is suitable for this assimilation with its peak surrounded by four spurs. More than sixty shrines of varying importance, and all very difficult to reach, were built on the mountainside; one bears the date equivalent to 1414. In most cases, the shrines consist of a break in the rock arranged as a cella with a terrace in front forming two or three tiers on the slope.

Candi Sukuh (on Mount Lawu half way between Solo and Tawangmangu) was built about 1430. It is a truncated pyramid facing west resting on three tiered terraces, crossed on the main east-west axis by three entrance pavilions. The lower pavilion has erotic symbols carved in relief on the paving. Near the southern stairway leading to the third terrace is a relief showing the god Ganesha in the forge where kris are being made. Candi Ceto (also on Mount Lawu, about seven kilometres north of Candi Sukuh: Plate 22) was built about 1470. It consists of an ill-defined shrine built on seven terraces. Each is divided into several tiers and many would have had wooden pavilions. This monument is not in its original state because it underwent a major restoration recently in an attempt to give it its former appearance. As a result, not all the restored elements correspond to those existing before the restoration. Even so, the monument, if different, shows the architecture has remained alive and blends perfectly with the Javanese countryside.

Candi Ceto was the last important temple built for the Hindu religion in Java, where the great Indian religions barely survived under the pressure of Islam.

8

The Architectural Perception of
Javanese Temples

JAVANESE temples should not be considered as symbolic enigmas where every stone takes on a particular significance. The temples are, however, the framework for conducting rites which are indeed symbolic. In the galleries in Borobudur, when a believer follows the panels representing the life of the Buddha, he copies this life and the monument takes on an entirely different value.

The temple is the dwelling where the god, whoever he is, resides on Mount Meru, and refers back to the conception of the universe which the Indianized world holds (Figure 20). Mount Meru comprises five summits; the stars move around the mountain, and its fabulous height, calculated by the Brahmins, is the equivalent of 1 344 000 kilometres. At its base, the mountain is surrounded by seven circular chains of mountains separated by seven oceans where marine monsters, the makaras, play. Beyond, to the south, in an eighth ocean is our pear-shaped world, the Jambudwipa, with in its centre Lake Anavatpa from where the four huge rivers flow to irrigate the world. In this same oceanic area are three other continents inhabited by strange beings with completely circular, crescent-shaped or entirely square heads. Finally, at an equally prodigious distance is the girdle of the universe, the Chakravan mountains, composed of rock crystal.

This is the Buddhist cosmogony and there are variations between different texts. Sometimes, for example, the faces of the inhabitants are not circular, crescent-shaped or square, but the continents themselves have these forms. Hinduism represents the universe in a slightly different way: Meru is the centre of the

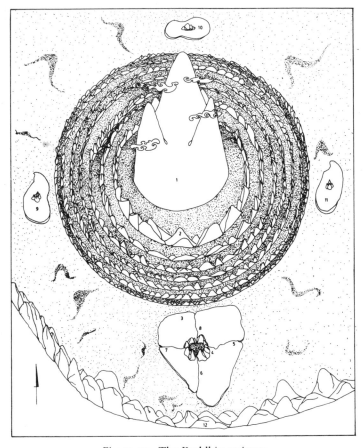

Figure 20. The Buddhist universe

1	Mount Meru	7	The Oxus
2	The seven chains of mountains and the seven oceans around them	8	The Tarim
3	Jambudwipa, the world in which we live	9	The world of round-faced creatures
		10	The world of crescent-faced creatures
4	Lake Anavatpa	11	The world of square-faced creatures
5	The Ganges	12	The chain of quartz mountains, Chakravan, completely surrounding the universe
6	The Indus		

continent which humans live on. The abode of Brahma is found at its summit and the gods dwell there, while all around celestial beings are transported in flying palaces.

It is hardly possible to express this universe in a realistic way, so the architectural forms are completely abstract. Only the decoration makes frequent allusions to its conceptual origin. In this way, at Candi Kidal (see Chapter 6), to eliminate any ambiguity in the meaning of the monument, the sculptors depicted allusions to the creation of the world under the direction of the god Visnu. It is with the aid of Mount Meru that the gods, tussling with the demons, churned the sea of milk from which the world came. A fabulous serpent wrapped itself around the mountain, the gods taking its head and the demons its tail, pulling alternately at each end and giving movement to the huge mountain.

The gods inhabit caves hollowed out in the sides of Mount Meru, so numerous sanctuaries in India were hollowed out in solid rock. In order for these caves to look like dwellings, architectural elements were carved into them and sometimes real elements of beamwork were inserted into the rock. This cavernous past largely formed the model of the Indian temple and so also of the Javanese temple, not only aesthetically but also technically. Certain methods of bonding stones had no other purpose but to find the cohesion of the original mountain to allow sculptors to work on a solid mass.

The Hindu-Javanese king was only partly divine; he was not an image of the god in its totality with all its superhuman powers. He played a defined role individualized in a particular location which was considered to be the image of the space where the god's power held sway. So the destiny of the king, at the same time his strength, had a function in the development of the divinity itself and after his death the king reverted to what he was the embodiment of. The temple constructed to shelter the statue showing him in his divine form was indeed Mount Meru, but it was also the dwelling of the sovereign in the centre of his realm, the enclosures and annexes of the temple becoming a refined scale model of the kingdom. The Buddhist king was more simply a Bodhisattva who, as such, came to the aid of his subjects, assuring them of the means of escaping from the cycle of rebirth. The inscriptions of the Khmer Buddhist king Jayavarman VII, at the beginning of the thirteenth century, are quite explicit on this point. The dead king, through his merits, became a Buddha and continued to watch over his kingdom; the temple constructed after his death was, like that of the Hindu king, a sort of ideal scale model representing a broad section of the universe.

This interpretation of the temple, its imaginary value, sometimes causes one to forget that the shrine was built to be admired. The believer crossing the threshold should be able to say that the architecture was worthy of the god it housed. This was a constant preoccupation and led to efforts of proportion which are extremely varied, both in relation to the general outline and also the main elements. The variations of these relationships in any one building cause changes in the way it is perceived by the attentive beholder and give vitality to the architecture.

The general outline was essentially traced to block the sunlight and had few structural functions. The plinth protected the base of the wall, but it also received the full force of the light, so it was often topped by a moulding whose two contrary curves gave variety, according to the time of the day, to the shadow produced by the play of reflected light on the stone or plaster coating. There is a tremendous variation in the outline of the inverted mouldings; depending on the location of the centre forming the outline, a moulding can be obtained which receives little sunlight (1 in Figure 20), no sunlight at all (2 in Figure 21) or, on the contrary, plenty of light (3 in Figure 21). When a builder introduced an inverted moulding which projected a great deal (2 in Figure 21), he obtained a kind of horizontal break in the building and the detail of the general outline can completely disappear if it cannot be viewed from the right distance, which is only possible if the spectator voluntarily steps back. When the temple is sufficiently large for the mouldings themselves to take on a certain volume, this disadvantage is no longer apparent, as the shadows will be varied by the play of light on the lower levels.

The architectural view varies considerably with the height of the sun, not only in relation to the detail of the moulding but also in relation to the main elements. For example, the choice of a cruciform plan was necessitated by iconographic reasons, but from this limitation the builders were able to enhance the appearance of the foreground. When this is in full light, it is always against a dark background caused by the shadow thrown by the projection of the arms of the cross.

The architecture of Javanese temples is skilful. It requires the beholder to move between different required viewpoints (the entrances through the enclosures, for example), to appreciate the effects of perspective which do not become coherent except at a fairly close distance to the building, some ten to fifteen metres. Because of the difficulty in anticipating the way the buildings were viewed, there were constant references to earlier buildings and this sometimes presupposes a considerable architectural knowledge on the part of the builders.

The ruinous state of the enclosures now makes it possible to see the monuments from points where originally they were hidden or only partly visible. In this way, Candi Siva at Prambanan could not be completely seen beyond the second enclosure. The major part of the main building was hidden by the walls and the three rows of Candi Perwara; only the false storeys and the finial were apparent. The many Candi Perwara were only designed to be seen close to and no distancing from them was possible between the different rows. In East Java,

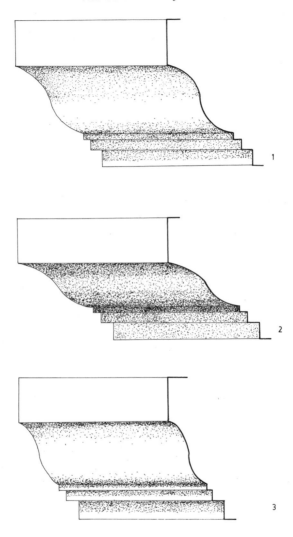

Figure 21. Variation in the effect of shade on different outlines of mouldings in the same light

Candi Kidal, in spite of its great height, was designed to be seen close to, as the enclosure, now reduced to a few foundation courses, partially obscured the building.

It can be seen that to appreciate Javanese temple architecture, a visitor is required to be able to reconstruct the original setting, as the temples have usually lost all their context and also their plastering. They now appear black, grey or red, but were covered with a white plastering and with colour added in many parts. The doors were of carved wood and were probably like contemporary Balinese temple doors. Tridents in gilded bronze topped the Sivaite temples and wheels of law the Buddhist temples. Inside, the statues were dressed and bedecked in jewels (jewels from the statues can be seen in the treasure house in the National Museum in Jakarta). The cellas were lit by oil lamps during ceremonies.

The architectural history of the monuments requires some attention even if, as in Borobudur, successive master builders were able to give the monument a cohesive aspect. The structure left by each previous builder influenced the architectural future of the building and its course was thus profoundly modified. For example, the cornice on the top of the wall of the first gallery at Borobudur was conceived for the first state of the monument in relation to perspective effects which the architect of the second state did not keep; today this element seems rightly to be somewhat out of proportion.

Finally, successive restorations of the monuments have fixed, sometimes unfortunately, aspects of the monuments which owe a lot to the imagination of the restorer (the finial of Candi Pawon is an example). The recent work at Borobudur and Prambanan has been more faithful, but sometimes, for excellent reasons of economy, the restoration has involved solutions which are not rigorously exact. In this way, the upper part of Borobudur is eighty centimetres below its original level, but for the present it is not practicable to reconstitute the circular terraces which were reasonably well restored in 1911. These eighty centimetres have had to be distributed among the heights of the more recently restored galleries, which explains in particular the positioning of the gully of some gargoyles above the paving. This anomaly will certainly be eliminated the day when the upper terraces are restored again. In the same way, the hill on which the monument has been built was arranged in levels which four enormous stairways cut across so that the upper plateau could be reached. Borobudur, instead of having a somewhat squashed appearance, looked completely different when the hill was entirely incorporated into the architecture.

This effort of imagination and attention required of a visitor will have its rewards in a better understanding, not to say discovery, of the creative work of the old Javanese master builders.

Chronology of
Monuments Mentioned

THE dates in italic are confirmed by epigraphical records. The different states of the Buddhist monuments of the eighth and ninth centuries are indicated at the end of Chapter 2. All the dates in this list and in the text are in the Christian era (AD), but the dates carved on the monuments are given in the Caka era, which started in 78.

early 8th century	Dieng: Arjuna, Semar, Srikandi, Gatokaca
+/− 750	Dieng: Puntadeva, Sembrodo, Bima, Gedong Songo Group II–VIII, Badut I
+/− 775	Borobudur I
778	Kalasan I
+/− 780	Sewu I
+/− 790	Kalasan II, Borobudur II, Lumbung I, Sajiwan I
792	Sewu II
+/− 810	Borobudur III, Kalasan III, Sewu III, Lumbung II, Sajiwan II
835/856	Prambanan
+/− 835	Borobudur IV–V, Gedong Songo Group I, Sambisari, Badut II, Kuning, Banon, Sari, Plaosan
+/− 950	Belahan I
977	Jalatunda I
+/− 1000	Gua Gajah (Bali)
1049	Belahan II
end 11th century	Gunung Kawi (Bali)
12th century	Gurah
+/− 1230	Sawentar
1239	Bara
+/− 1250	Badut: last alterations
+/− 1260	Kidal
+/− 1280	Jago

end 13th century		Singosari, Jawi
1343		Jago: alterations
+/.−	1347	Penataran: main terrace
+/−	1350	all structures built near Trowulan, Jalatunda II
1354		Jabung
1369		Penataran: dated temple, Gayatri
+/−	1370	Teguwangi
1371		Pari
1375		Penataran: pendopo terrace
+/−	1375	Belahan III, Gunung Gansir
1389		Gayatri: remodelling
+/−	1390	Surowono
1414		Temple LXI on Mount Penangunggan
+/−	1430	Sukuh
+/−	1470	Ceto

Glossary

Antefix: a repeated ornament at the lowest level of the roof

Balustrade: an ornamental parapet or low wall to a terrace

Body of building: the lower part of a temple, raised on the foundation and supporting the false storeys above (2 in Figure 4)

Cella: internal space of a temple, usually containing a statue

Corbel: a projection jutting out from a wall to support weight

Cornice: a horizontal moulded projection above the body of a building

Door casing: the whole woodwork frame including the bronze hinges, etc. for a door or window

Entablature: the three parts comprising the top of a wall (the architrave, the frieze and the cornice); in Javanese buildings these three parts are rarely all present and the frieze or the architrave are often omitted

Finial or capping: the topmost part of the tower (6 in Figure 4)

Gable end: the side end of a roof with two panels; when the gable end tilts outwards it is referred to as overhanging (for example, in the case of the beamwork of the ridges in tension, Figures 10, 11, 12)

Module: a unit measurement by which the proportions of a building are regulated

Mortar (binding agent): in Java, a mixture of lime, sand and water. In the ninth century the proportions were usually two parts of lime for three parts of sand, sometimes reduced to only two parts. From the thirteenth century a binding agent most likely consisting of plant sap and sugar was used.

Moulding: the cyma recta or doucine, a double-curved moulding, concave above and convex below (Figure 21)

Outline: the whole ensemble of mouldings of a building or one of its parts (the outline of the base or the cornice is the ensemble of mouldings of these elements)

Pediment: the triangular part crowning the front of a building, especially over a portico

Pilaster: a rectangular column, usually forming part of the wall

Plinth: the lower square member of the base of a column, or the lowest projecting part of the base of a building

Porch or portico: the element of a building forming its entrance (12 in Figure 4)

Ridge: the horizontal part forming the top of the roof; when the ridge is in tension, it does not rest on trusses, but the weight of the projecting gable ends keeps it in position

Stepped reduction of roofline: the receding part of the temple roof forming the tower, each level of the false storey above reproducing on a smaller scale that below it (11 in Figure 4)

String wall: the wall framing a stairway (10 in Figure 4)

Stucco: a simple mortar of lime and sand

Truss: the supporting structure of the roof

Bibliography

In order to understand the architecture of Javanese temples better, and the research which preceded restoration work, the Dutch review *Oudheidkundig Verslag* should be consulted. This appeared quarterly (sometimes with different numbers grouped together) from 1913 to 1950, with an interruption during the war. After 1950 the Indonesian department of archaeology continued the Dutch publications under different titles, the main ones being *Bulletin of the Research Centre of Archaeology*, *Berita Penelitian Arkeologi*, *Amerta* and *Arkeologi*. The organization which supervised the restoration of Candi Borobudur published an interesting collection of small books relating to different aspects of the work, under a single common title, *Pelita Borobudur*.

Bernet-Kempers, A. J., *Ancient Indonesian Art*, Amsterdam, 1959.

———— *Herstel in eigen waarde monumentenzorg in Indonesia*, Den Haag, 1978.

Bosch, F. D. K., *Selected studies in Indonesian archaeology*, The Hague, 1961.

de Casparis, J. G., *Inscripties uit de Cailendra tijd* (Prasasti Indonesia I), Bandung, 1950.

———— *Selected inscriptions from the 7th to the 9th century A.D.* (Prasasti Indonesia II), Bandung, 1956.

Dumarçay, J. (translated and edited by M. Smithies), *Borobudur*, Kuala Lumpur, 1978.

———— *Candi Sewu et l'architecture bouddhique du centre de Java*, Paris, 1982.

Galestine, Th. P., *Houtbow op oost jawansche tempelreliefs*, 1936.

Pigeaud, Th., *Java in the 14th century*, *I–V*, The Hague, 1960–3.

Stutterheim, T., *Studies in Indonesian archaeology*, The Hague, 1956.

Van Erp, T., *Barabudur architectural description*, The Hague, 1931.

Vlekke, B. H. M., *Nusantara, a history of Indonesia*, The Hague, 1960.

Some other Oxford Paperbacks for readers interested in Central Asia, China and South-East Asia, past and present

CAMBODIA

GEORGE COEDÈS
Angkor: An Introduction

CENTRAL ASIA

PETER FLEMING
Bayonets to Lhasa

LADY MACARTNEY
An English Lady in Chinese
Turkestan

ALBERT VON LE COQ
Buried Treasures of Chinese
Turkestan

AITCHEN WU
Turkistan Tumult

CHINA

HAROLD ACTON
Peonies and Ponies

ERNEST BRAMAH
Kai Lung's Golden Hours

ANN BRIDGE
The Ginger Griffin

PETER FLEMING
The Siege at Peking

CORRINNE LAMB
The Chinese Festive Board

W. SOMERSET MAUGHAM
On a Chinese Screen*

G. E. MORRISON
An Australian in China

OSBERT SITWELL
Escape with Me! An Oriental
Sketch-book

INDONESIA

S. TAKDIR ALISJAHBANA
Indonesia: Social and Cultural
Revolution

DAVID ATTENBOROUGH
Zoo Quest for a Dragon*

VICKI BAUM
A Tale from Bali

MIGUEL COVARRUBIAS
Island of Bali*

BERYL DE ZOETE AND
WALTER SPIES
Dance and Drama in Bali

AUGUSTA DE WIT
Java: Facts and Fancies

JACQUES DUMARCAY
Borobudur

JACQUES DUMARCAY
The Temples of Java

JENNIFER LINDSAY
Javanese Gamelan

EDWIN M. LOEB
Sumatra: Its History and People

MOCHTAR LUBIS
Twilight in Djakarta

MADELON H. LULOFS
Coolie*

ANNA MATHEWS
The Night of Purnama

COLIN McPHEE
A House in Bali*

HICKMAN POWELL
The Last Paradise

E. R. SCIDMORE
Java, Garden of the East

MICHAEL SMITHIES
Yogyakarta

LADISLAO SZÉKELY
Tropic Fever: The Adventures of
a Planter in Sumatra

EDWARD C. VAN NESS AND
SHITA PRAWIROHARDJO
Javanese Wayang Kulit

MALAYSIA

ABDULLAH ABDUL KADIR
The Hikayat Abdullah

ISABELLA L. BIRD
The Golden Chersonese: Travels
in Malaya in 1879

PIERRE BOULLE
Sacrilege in Malaya

MARGARET BROOKE
RANEE OF SARAWAK
My Life in Sarawak

C. C. BROWN (Editor)
Sejarah Melayu or Malay Annals

COLIN N. CRISSWELL
Rajah Charles Brooke: Monarch
of All He Surveyed

K. M. ENDICOTT
An Analysis of Malay Magic

HENRI FAUCONNIER
The Soul of Malaya

W. R. GEDDES
Nine Dayak Nights

JOHN D. GIMLETTE
Malay Poisons and Charm Cures

JOHN D. GIMLETTE AND
H. W. THOMSON
A Dictionary of Malayan
Medicine

A. G. GLENISTER
The Birds of the Malay Peninsula,
Singapore and Penang

C. W. HARRISON
Illustrated Guide to the Federated
Malay States (1923)

TOM HARRISSON
World Within: A Borneo Story

DENNIS HOLMAN
Noone of the Ulu

CHARLES HOSE
The Field-Book of a Jungle-Wallah

SYBIL KATHIGASU
No Dram of Mercy

MALCOLM MacDONALD
Borneo People

SOMERSET MAUGHAM
The Casuarina Tree*

AMBROSE B. RATHBORNE
Camping and Tramping in Malaya

ROBERT W. C. SHELFORD
A Naturalist in Borneo

J. T. THOMSON
Glimpses into Life in Malayan Land

RICHARD WINSTEDT
The Malay Magician

PHILIPPINES

AUSTIN COATES
Rizal

SINGAPORE

PATRICK ANDERSON
Snake Wine: A Singapore Episode

ROLAND BRADDELL
The Lights of Singapore

R. W. E. HARPER AND
HARRY MILLER
Singapore Mutiny

JANET LIM
Sold for Silver

G. M. REITH
Handbook to Singapore (1907)

J. D. VAUGHAN
The Manners and Customs of the
Chinese of the Straits Settlements

C. E. WURTZBURG
Raffles of the Eastern Isles

THAILAND

CARL BOCK
Temples and Elephants

REGINALD CAMPBELL
Teak-Wallah

MALCOLM SMITH
A Physician at the Court of Siam

ERNEST YOUNG
The Kingdom of the Yellow Robe

Titles marked with an asterisk have restricted rights